Playing the Assassin
Assassin
by
David Robson

For Seth Reichgott and Joe Brancato,
two of the finest coaches I know.

Playing the Assassin
© David Robson
Trade Edition, 2017
ISBN 978-1-63092-101-9

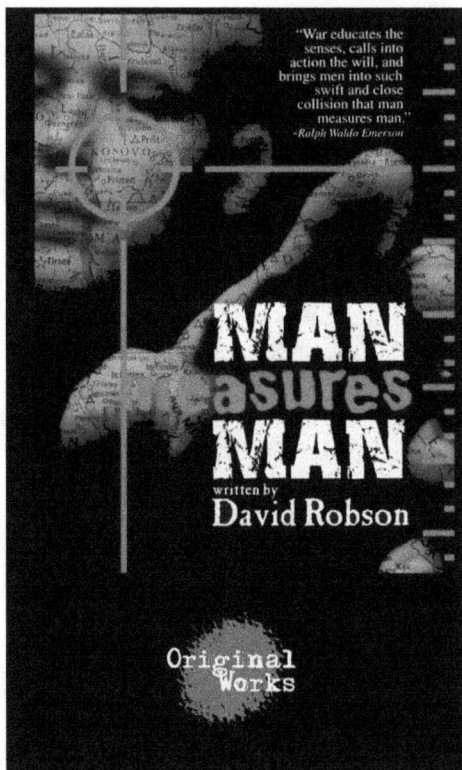

MAN MEASURES MAN

Synopsis: In the waning days of the Kosovo conflict, two American doctors travel to Macedonia to offer their services to Albanian refugees. Into the chaos of the medical camp, a mysterious boy arrives, forcing the doctors to re-examine their actions and the personal ethics that guide them.

Cast Size: 4 Males, 2 Females

Assassin was first produced in Philadelphia, Pennsylvania, in a co-production by InterAct Theatre Company (Seth Rozin, Founder and Producing Artistic Director; Anneliese Van Arsdale, Managing Director) and Act II Playhouse (Tony Braithwaite, Artistic Director; Howie Brown, Managing Director). Performances began on January 18, 2013. The director was Seth Reichgott; the set was designed by Dirk Durossette, the costumes were designed by Maggie Baker, the lighting was designed by James Leitner, the sound was designed by Ashley Turner, the fight choreography was by Mike Consenza; the stage manager was Tom Helmer. The cast was as follows:

FRANK   Brian Anthony Wilson

LEWIS   Dwayne A. Thomas

Playing the Assassin, a revised version of the play, was first produced in Stony Point, New York, by Penguin Rep Theatre (Joe Brancato, artistic director; Andrew M. Horn, Executive Director). Performances began on September 19, 2014. The director was Joe Brancato. The scenic design was by Brian Prather, the costumes were designed by Charlotte Palmer-Lane, the lighting was designed by Ed McCarthy, the sound was designed by Emily Auciello, the fight choreography was designed by Christopher Plummer; the stage manager was Michael Palmer. The cast was as follows:

LEWIS   Garrett Lee Hendricks

FRANK   Ezra Knight

"A man goes far to find out what he is."
—Theodore Roethke

CHARACTERS

FRANK, *African American ex-professional football player, fifties*

LEWIS, *African American television producer, thirties*

SETTING
Hotel room, Chicago, Illinois

TIME
Present

NOTE
Playing the Assassin works best when actors and director view it as a "fight for yardage," as in the game of professional football. The characters study each other, prowl the field of battle, look for openings in their opponent's defenses, and fight to stand their ground. Still, if the play is viewed simply as a "football play," the proverbial woods and trees may be missed completely. Ultimately, these men are fighting for their lives and a chance at redemption. Beyond that, the play should be performed for maximum intensity.

PLAYING THE ASSASSIN

(Lights rise on a mid-price hotel suite. Door, up right, leads to a hallway. This is the living room part of the suite, with a sofa, chair, coffee table, small refrigerator, and television. A jacket is flung over the chair; a glass and a pill bottle [a mini bottle of booze] sit on the coffee table, [along with a row of pill bottles]. A cane stands in a corner. Upstage center is an open doorway that leads to the bedroom and bathroom. The television, which does not face the audience, is loud—a football game. LEWIS, in a suit, stands center holding his briefcase.)

FRANK *(Off)*:   Sorry I'm running a little late: Lost track of time.

LEWIS: It's not a problem.

(LEWIS looks around the room, examining the booze, the pill bottles.)

FRANK *(Off)*:   I'll be there in a minute.

LEWIS: Take your time.

FRANK *(Off)*:   Have a seat. Help yourself to a drink.

LEWIS: I'm fine, thanks.

FRANK *(Off)*: Whatever you say!

LEWIS: When did you get in?

FRANK *(Off)*: About an hour ago.

LEWIS: From San Francisco?

(FRANK enters from the bedroom.)

FRANK: From Oakland.

LEWIS: I didn't realize Oakland had an airport.

FRANK: Oh, yeah, got all kinds of things in Oakland now: gas stations, hospitals, Targets… I'm messing with you.

LEWIS: That's funny.

FRANK: I like to joke around sometimes: puts people at ease, you know?

LEWIS: Pleasure to meet you, sir.

FRANK: Thank you.

LEWIS: I hope your room is satisfactory?

FRANK: It's fine—kind of nice, actually. Still, you won't see the younger guys today staying in a place like this. They only go five stars. Something to drink before we go?

LEWIS: What are you having?

FRANK: Oh, me? Just a soda—not a drinker. You?

LEWIS: Juice is fine.

(FRANK goes to mini bar, returns, eyes on the TV, and hands LEWIS a bottle of juice. FRANK un-mutes the TV.)

FRANK: Would you look at that? Patriots again. They're making this look easy. Who you rooting for?

LEWIS: No preference really.

(FRANK turns down the volume on the TV.)

FRANK: But these are the playoffs, baby. Only come once a year. You got like somebody.

LEWIS: The Ravens have had a good season.

FRANK: Hell yes, they have.

LEWIS: Tough year for your old team the Raiders, though.

FRANK: Worst record in the NFL.

LEWIS: That's too bad.

FRANK: An embarrassment! But, once a Raider, always a Raider.

LEWIS: A different story from when you played.

FRANK: Tell me about it. *(FRANK checks his watch.)* Hey, I guess we better get downstairs—don't want to keep them all waiting.

LEWIS: What's that?

FRANK: This is a meet-and-greet, right?

LEWIS: I don't know what you mean.

FRANK: You bring in the network brass, we all shoot the shit, you guys blow a little smoke up my ass, and then we get this thing done.

LEWIS: Oh, no, it's nothing like that.

FRANK: So what is it?

LEWIS: I'm here to finalize plans and conduct a pre-interview with you.

FRANK: Just the two of us…

LEWIS: Yes, if that's alright.

FRANK: It's just that on the phone you gave me the impression that this was a big deal…

LEWIS: As far as CBS is concerned it is a very big deal. We're doing an interview piece on the two of you that will be shown in the hour prior to the Super Bowl itself. We're still in the planning stages, but we'll most likely have a host asking you questions in front of massive photos from your playing days.

FRANK: I like the sound of that.

LEWIS: I'm thinking it'll begin with some kind of montage from your games and intersperse interviews with each of you separately. Then, at some point, we'll show the two of you together.

FRANK: Together?

LEWIS: It's a reunion, after all.

FRANK: But what if he doesn't, you know…

LEWIS: What?

FRANK: What if he won't...? I don't want to upset the man.

LEWIS: What's most important is that the two of you meet face-to-face. What happens next is up to you.

FRANK: I guess you're right. And hey, whatever heightens the drama and shit. Drum roll, please, right?

LEWIS: That's right.

FRANK: Damn, Super Bowl pre-game!

LEWIS: It's a big showcase.

FRANK: The biggest! We'll light up the night sky, baby—ratings through the roof.

LEWIS: That's the plan.

FRANK: What are you going to call it?

LEWIS: Call it—?

FRANK: You've got to give it a name—some kind of tagline to sell this thing.

LEWIS: Usually the marketing department takes care of—

FRANK: Call it something like, uh...uh...I got it: "Reunion of the Legends." What do you think?

LEWIS: I don't know if it's quite accurate.

FRANK: Sure, it's accurate—

LEWIS: Lyle Turner was injured during his second season.

FRANK: So what? It sounds good; that's all that matters.

LEWIS: I guess a little hyperbole couldn't hurt.

FRANK: A one-time, never-before-seen reunion between two of the NFL's greatest players!

LEWIS: Two decades in the making.

FRANK: Yeah, but who's counting, right?

LEWIS: Aren't you?

FRANK: What's that supposed to mean? Why should I be counting?

LEWIS: No reason. I'm just making conversation.

FRANK: Once something's done, it's done—no looking back.

LEWIS: I'm sure you're right.

FRANK: What is it you do for CBS exactly?

LEWIS: I'm a segment producer. I do the leg work—make the contacts, set up interviews, all the behind-the-scenes stuff.

FRANK: Yeah, and the on-air guys take all the credit.

LEWIS: That's okay; I prefer being the research guy.

FRANK: Shy type, huh?

LEWIS: I've just learned, over time, where the power really lies. They report the stories, but I write the stories. Those talking heads don't say a word unless they get it from me.

FRANK: Then I guess calling me was your idea.

LEWIS: Yes. It's a great human interest story.

FRANK: You got that right.

LEWIS: The NFL tried to bury what happened between you and Lyle Turner. It was a black eye on the sport, a tragedy that they wanted to forget about as quickly as possible.

FRANK: So why not keep it buried?

LEWIS: The drama needs an ending, doesn't it?

FRANK: What'd you have in mind?

LEWIS: How it ends really isn't up to me, Mr. Baker.

FRANK: I guess not.

LEWIS: The ball's in your court, as it were.

FRANK: Yeah, but see, I don't play tennis.

LEWIS: No, you prefer contact sports.

FRANK: I like fucking people up.

LEWIS: I'll have to remember that. Listen, I'm sorry this
is all so last minute.

FRANK: No problem at all.

LEWIS: But the Super Bowl is two weeks away. We
have to get this done tonight, or it just isn't going to
happen.

FRANK: I'm easy to work with, believe me. It's the other
guy you need to worry about.

LEWIS: That's already taken care of. We reached out to Mr. Turner last week.

FRANK: Oh, yeah? What'd he say?

LEWIS: He's interested.

FRANK: You talked to him directly?

LEWIS: We did.

FRANK: Everybody has a price, don't they? And when the network calls you, you answer.

LEWIS: It's now or never, isn't it? Neither of you is getting any younger.

FRANK: We're not that old, son.

LEWIS: No, but you likely don't have another twenty years to sort this out.

FRANK: I feel you; I feel you right there. You, uh, ready to get going?

LEWIS: Sure, just let me finish this. Are you in a hurry?

FRANK: No, no, not at all. Take your time.

LEWIS: Thanks.

FRANK: Do you mind if we, uh, we talk [about] money while we got a few minutes?

LEWIS: We can talk about anything you want.

FRANK: 'Cause we *are* talking a payday, aren't we?

LEWIS: CBS does not make a habit of paying for its interviews, but considering the extraordinary nature of this story, the network is willing to offer each of you $100,000.

FRANK: One hundred thousand...

LEWIS: You don't sound happy.

FRANK: This shit is exclusive.

LEWIS: The cost of broadcasting the Super Bowl is very expensive.

FRANK: Don't give me no song and dance, "we have no money", bullshit, now. It's the biggest event on TV every year. Advertisers pay millions. You can squeeze a little more money out of your bosses if you really want to. I'm negotiating for Lyle, too, you know? Whatever I get, he gets.

LEWIS: He's lucky to have you looking out for him.

FRANK: That's what I'm saying.

LEWIS: Then again, some might say it's the least you can do.

FRANK: Huh?

LEWIS: The man's in a wheelchair.

FRANK: Hold on, now. I didn't come here for no hatchet job.

LEWIS: There's no reason to get defensive. I was simply stating a fact.

FRANK: Yeah, but see, whenever guys like you call me, they start by asking things like, "Mr. Baker, do you miss playing football?"; "Mr. Baker, what made you such a hard hitter?"; "Mr. Baker, tell us what you think of all the head injuries." But all that's a build-up to the big one: "Mr. Baker, do you have any regrets about what you did to Lyle Turner?" What I did—like I'm a Nazi or something, like I committed a crime.

LEWIS: I thought I made it very clear that this is to be about the play that injured Mr. Turner—

FRANK: That's all you want to talk about? I had a whole career—

LEWIS: No, but it has to be a key part of the interview—

FRANK: Says who?

LEWIS: Says me, says CBS. It's all right here in the contract.

(LEWIS takes a contract from his briefcase.)

FRANK: Contract...?

LEWIS: That's right.

FRANK: You didn't mention any contract on the phone.

LEWIS: I think I did.

FRANK: You didn't.

LEWIS: Well, I have it here now. Take a few minutes to read it.

FRANK: I don't read contracts; my lawyers do.

LEWIS: We need an answer tonight.

FRANK: Tell you what: you show me some cash, I sign it right now. No cash, no sign.

LEWIS: It doesn't work that way.

FRANK: Then educate me, Mr. Segment Producer.

LEWIS: You sign; I sign; I take it back to the network; and on the day of your appearance you receive payment.

FRANK: What, no signing bonus?

LEWIS: I'm afraid not. It's not like football.

FRANK: How the hell would you know?

LEWIS: I'm talking about the TV end of things.

FRANK: I don't like this. I don't like this one bit.

LEWIS: Is that a requirement, Mr. Baker?

FRANK: No, but I see how it is.

LEWIS: How what is?

FRANK: You fly me out here to Chicago, get me a nice room, but it sounds like you're just looking to take me down.

LEWIS: That's not it at all.

FRANK: What is it, then?

LEWIS: We just want the truth.

FRANK: That's what they all say. See, I meet people like you all the time.

LEWIS: People like me?

FRANK: You come in here with your tailored suit and flashy cuff links and try to shove some kind of shady deal down my throat—

LEWIS: Take a look. I assure you that this is standard policy.

FRANK: I don't like surprises.

(FRANK thumbs through the contract, not looking closely.)

LEWIS: That was an unfortunate miscommunication—

FRANK: You can say that again.

LEWIS: We're presenting you with an opportunity, Mr. Baker.

FRANK: So I have no say in any of this.

LEWIS: It's our show; it's our money. Now, we can end this right here if you'd like, if you're uncomfortable.

FRANK: I didn't say I was uncomfortable, but I want to know, you know, what kind of stuff you're going to ask me before I think about putting anything in writing.

LEWIS: Then perhaps we should get on with the pre-interview. We'll deal with the contract later. Is that alright with you?

FRANK: Yeah, fine, fine.

LEWIS: Where would you like to do it? How about over here?

FRANK *(Looking at TV)*: How about a little "D" Ravens...? Aw, look at that. They got holes like Swiss fucking cheese in that defense. Tighten up, tighten up!

(LEWIS takes out his cell phone, fiddles with it.)

LEWIS: I'm going to record this. Would you mind muting that?

(FRANK uses the remote to lower the TV sound further.)

FRANK: Do what you have to do.

LEWIS: Would you have a seat, please?

(FRANK explores the mini-bar, finds some snacks: pretzels, chips, candy bars.)

FRANK: I thought you were buying me dinner. Wasn't that the plan?

LEWIS: Yes, but this might be better.

FRANK: Not for me. I see they got a nice restaurant in the hotel.

LEWIS: We need a quiet place.

FRANK: Yeah, but see, I can't eat this shit—I got the sugar. I need something a little more, you know, substantial. I mean, ain't you hungry?

LEWIS: I can wait.

FRANK: Maybe we can do room service then. *(FRANK finds a menu.)* Let's see, what have we got here? *(FRANK scans the menu.)* I'm thinking a cheeseburger, maybe, or the Cobb salad...

LEWIS: I'd go with salad, if I were you.

FRANK: Why's that?

LEWIS: I don't eat ground beef anymore.

FRANK: Why not?

LEWIS: You never know what the hell is in it.

FRANK: Sure you do: Beef.

LEWIS: I'm saying the cattle industry is not in the best shape right now. I probably shouldn't be telling you this.

FRANK: Tell me.

LEWIS: It's just that with all these factory farms they have so many millions of heads of cattle—most of them getting sick from eating the corn they're fed.

FRANK: What's wrong with corn?

LEWIS: Well, physiologically, the bovine body isn't built to eat corn; it's built to eat grass. So, the animals get sick and farmers shoot them full of steroids and antibiotics, and before you know it they're rendering these broken down cows and grinding them into the patties we're—well, *you're*—eating.

FRANK: That's fucked up. Still, a man has got to eat, Lewis. Maybe we could order out—Chinese or something. What do you say?

LEWIS: That's not what I came for.

FRANK: All business, huh?

LEWIS: It shouldn't take long. We'll do this and I'll take you out for a nice steak.

FRANK: I guess we're staying then.

(FRANK eats another cookie and sits.)

FRANK: How'd you know all that?

LEWIS: All what?

FRANK: You know, about the cattle.

LEWIS: I read.

FRANK: You know what I read? I read the sports pages, and all these years later you guys in the media still paint Lyle Turner and me as enemies, but I have no doubt that if circumstances had been different, Lyle and I might have been friends.

LEWIS: You think so?

FRANK: Stranger things have happened.

LEWIS: Okay now, I want to start with a couple of establishing questions—just to make sure I have some of the basic facts straight. *(LEWIS begins recording their conversation.)* This is a pre-interview with Frank Baker, recorded on January 19 *(Checks his watch)* at 7:21 pm. Just for background, you were an All-American at Nebraska.

FRANK: That's right.

LEWIS: The Oakland Raiders drafted you in 1979...

FRANK: Uh huh.

LEWIS: You played with them for ten years before being traded to the Bengals, where you played your final two years in the NFL.

FRANK: Anybody with half a brain can tell you that shit. I thought you said you were a research guy.

LEWIS: I am.

FRANK: Then prove it. I want to see how good you are. How many career interceptions I got? [do I have?]

LEWIS: Is this a test?

FRANK: Isn't everything?

LEWIS: What do I get if I pass?

FRANK: You get to play with the Assassin, baby.

LEWIS: What if I don't want to play?

FRANK: All you TV guys want to play. You want to peer behind the face mask, find out what made me the hardest-hitting, baddest motherfucker in the history of the NFL.

LEWIS: I just want to ask you some questions.

FRANK: Show me what you got, hotshot. You think you know all about what happened between me and Turner, so let's see what else you know. How many career interceptions do I have? Come on, humor me.

LEWIS: You had 66 career interceptions.

FRANK: Tackles?

LEWIS: 1231.

FRANK: How many games I play in?

LEWIS: 192.

FRANK: You got all that in your head?

LEWIS: I have a mind for numbers. Ask me who blocked the most passes in any year and I can tell you.

FRANK: 1962.

LEWIS: Ernie Reynolds with 12.

FRANK: How many passes I block in my career?

LEWIS: Safeties don't have the chance to block many passes, but you have a surprisingly high number: 7.

FRANK: Shit, brother, you know more about me than I know about myself.

LEWIS: Mr. Baker, there's a lot I don't know—a lot of things numbers can't tell you.

FRANK: Like what?

LEWIS: You played for 12 years, longer than most players—especially at your position. How'd you manage that and not get hurt?

FRANK: Yeah, and we took a bigger pounding back then when the pads were thinner, less able absorb a hit. As far as I'm concerned, they coddle players today. They're supposed to be better physical specimens, but what, they pull a hamstring and they're out for three weeks. They sprain their ankle—the whole season is lost. No, these guys couldn't play the kind of football I did. They'd all be carried off the field on stretchers. Not me; I knew how to play the game.

LEWIS: You got the chance.

FRANK: What are you talking about?

LEWIS: You tell me.

FRANK: I read offenses not minds.

LEWIS: You read them well. You were a take-no-prisoners kind of type—got off on laying men out.

FRANK: Got off how? You mean it turned me on or something? Where'd you read that?

LEWIS: Maybe I read it somewhere. Maybe I just made it up.

FRANK: That's okay: people used to make shit up about me all the time, but I thought you prided yourself on accuracy.

LEWIS: We all have our blind spots.

FRANK: You ever see me play?

LEWIS: Only on YouTube.

FRANK: What'd you see?

LEWIS: I saw the '83 Super Bowl when you hit Tommy Floyd so hard his helmet flew off.

FRANK: Let me tell you: my only regret is I did not hit Floyd hard enough. The son of a bitch still caught the ball.

LEWIS: But you won the Super Bowl.

FRANK: We won the Super Bowl, but football is a game of individual plays. If I could have that play back I'd truly knock the shit out of him.

LEWIS: You can't hit people like that anymore.

FRANK: What would they do—suspend me for a couple of games, dock me some pay?

LEWIS: The league can take serious action in extreme cases—

FRANK: What extreme cases?

LEWIS: Bounties—where a team pays its players extra to hurt people.

FRANK: All is fair in love, war, and football, my man, and bounties are nothing new. We did that shit all the time in the '70s and '80s. The only difference is now it's institutionalized. Back then, it was more like a bar bet. Anyway, what difference does it make? The game's about fucking people up—always has been, always will be. That's where people like me come in.

LEWIS: Tough guys, you mean.

FRANK: Damn straight. The NFL needs guys like me. Difference is today these young guys get all inked-up with these bad-ass tattoos, show up in magazines with their shirts off, guns out and oiled. These motherfuckers are the biggest celebrities on the planet. Talk about getting off on the game. I mean, there is such a thing as humility.

LEWIS: You're jealous.

FRANK: Not me, man. I did shit; I played.

LEWIS: Ancient history!

FRANK: I'm a legend, motherfucker! What did you ever do?

(LEWIS stops recording.)

LEWIS: We're supposed to be interviewing *you*, Mr. Baker.

FRANK: Yeah, but I'm turning the tables, like on *Law and Order* and shit. Now, let's hear it, Barack Obama: What did you do with your life? Press the button on your little smarty phone there; I want this for posterity.

(LEWIS turns the recorder on.)

LEWIS: You're putting me on the spot.

FRANK: Sneak attacks are my specialty. Wait, let me guess: Both your parents are doctors; bought you a black BMW for your sixteenth birthday; paid your way through college. Correct that: You were top of your class—maybe not first, but in the top five. That means all the big schools came calling on the smartest Negro in the room. Am I warm…?

LEWIS: Not even close.

FRANK: Sure I'm not. I had you pegged the moment you walked in the door. Guys like you talk a good game, but face it, brother: In your heart of hearts, people like you dream of being people like me.

LEWIS: Don't flatter yourself.

FRANK: You telling me I'm wrong?

LEWIS: You're wrong. I didn't look up to athletes.

FRANK: Oh, don't tell me: the people you looked up to rode buses through the Deep South, marched to Selma, right?

LEWIS: Are you mocking me, Mr. Baker?

FRANK: Hell yes, I'm mocking you. You want equal rights? Take a look at the NFL. That's where a black man goes to get his piece of the American dream these days. Most kids today don't have a clue about civil rights. Oh, they know Rosa Parks, right? Everybody knows Rosa fucking Parks. And King. But who else, huh? I'll tell you who: nobody. But they know people like me, don't they?

LEWIS: Yes.

FRANK: I can't hear you, son!

LEWIS: Yes!

FRANK: Damn right! See, people like me have the real power in this life because we serve a purpose.

LEWIS: Which is what?

FRANK: Football players make people happy. People pay a few bucks and in return they get to watch grown men hurt each other.

LEWIS: That makes people happy?

FRANK: Where you been living, boy? 'Course it does. People need it, you know? Like the Romans needed the gladiators. Society needs that release, or else you'll have a lot more murders and rapes and shit. Man is a violent creature by nature.

LEWIS: Give me a break.

FRANK: You want the truth? I'm giving you some.

LEWIS: Boys are taught to see athletes as role models— the bigger and tougher the better. And then when they grow up—

FRANK: Is that how you were raised?

LEWIS: It's how we're all raised.

FRANK: You speakin' for everybody now…?

LEWIS: We're here to talk about Lyle Turner.

FRANK: *You're* here to talk about Lyle Turner. Where'd you go to school?

LEWIS: Why does it matter?

FRANK: I want to know who I'm talking to.

LEWIS: I went to Howard.

FRANK: Howard. How long you been working for the network?

LEWIS: As a producer, you mean?

FRANK: No, as a lawn jockey! Yes, as a producer.

LEWIS: I don't know. Three years.

FRANK: Pay good...?

LEWIS: Mr. Baker.

FRANK: Call me Frank.

LEWIS *(After a beat)*: It's probably best if we keep it formal.

FRANK: Whatever you say, Mr. Producer! I just wanted to know how well the network paid you. But don't mind me: I often breach the bounds of propriety. Always did, always will.

LEWIS: It's really none of your business.

FRANK: Yeah, but like I said, I often breach the bounds—

LEWIS: — "Breach the bounds of propriety."

FRANK: —Of propriety. That's right. See, when I say it fancy that way it makes people laugh. Then they usually tell me the truth, or to fuck off.

LEWIS: Fuck off.

FRANK: Just like that! Yeah! Now tell me, uh, uh...

LEWIS: Lewis.

FRANK: Lewis!

LEWIS: Yes.

FRANK: Can I trust you?

LEWIS: How do you mean?

(FRANK switches off LEWIS' cell phone recorder.)

FRANK: I mean if I ask you something, can you keep it between us? This might sound like a funny question.

LEWIS: I'm listening.

FRANK: When you talked to Lyle, you know, on the phone, what did he call me?

LEWIS: Call you...?

FRANK: Yeah, you know, how did he refer to me? Did he use Frank, or Baker, or He Who Shall Not Be Named, or that son of a bitch who put me in this wheelchair?

LEWIS: I'd have to think about it.

FRANK: Think about it.

LEWIS: He may have referred to you as Baker a few times.

FRANK: Alright.

LEWIS: But mostly he didn't use a name. He used a pronoun. You know, "him," or "he."

FRANK: But you knew he meant me.

LEWIS: It's who you are to him, I suppose: this, this out-
line of a man that he can't completely fill in. Still,
you're there, you know, like a shadow hovering...but
never landing...

FRANK: What the fuck are you talking about?

LEWIS: What I mean is that you've been a part of his life
for a long time.

FRANK: You know, I read what he said about me.

LEWIS: When?

FRANK: A few years back—he gave an interview and
said how the injury had been a test of his faith and all,
and that he forgave me and shit. He didn't have to say
that.

LEWIS: He didn't have to say anything.

FRANK: Yeah, but he did. I appreciated that. How's he
doing--you know, health-wise?

LEWIS: He's dying.

FRANK: We're all dying, my man.

LEWIS: You look pretty healthy.

FRANK: Looks can be deceiving. Between the pills I take for blood pressure and the ones I take for my sciatica, and this damn cane, I'm a regular walking Walgreens. So, uh, what kind of time's Lyle looking at?

LEWIS: How should I know?

FRANK: I just thought that maybe he said something on the phone—

LEWIS: He didn't. Although I've read that people who have been paralyzed from the neck down barely live five-to-seven years after being hurt. He's outlived all predictions.

FRANK: Guess we've both lived long enough to be forgotten. That's got be some sort of accomplishment, right?

LEWIS: I couldn't tell you.

FRANK: You ever play?

LEWIS: What's that?

FRANK: As a kid or something—you ever play football?

LEWIS: I just watched.

FRANK: 'Cause you look kind of athletic. You got an athlete's frame.

LEWIS: I used to run a little bit.

FRANK: What—like track or something?

LEWIS: Yes, distance—800 meters.

FRANK: Not really a team sport, is it?

LEWIS: Not like football.

FRANK: But you liked it.

LEWIS: I liked the solitude of it, the loneliness—the time to be with your own thoughts, to not have to listen to anyone else, not have to, you know, do for anyone else, only yourself.

FRANK: Oh yeah?

LEWIS: I don't believe in taking out your aggression on other men. I mean, if you're going to punish someone it should be yourself.

FRANK: Not sure I could get into that.

LEWIS: We should get back to the business at hand.

FRANK: You have a favorite team?

LEWIS: Favorite—?

FRANK: A favorite football team as a kid—who'd you like?

LEWIS: I don't know.

FRANK: You know!

LEWIS: I liked the…the Steelers.

FRANK: Aw, now you're bullshitting me.

LEWIS: Why is that bullshit?

FRANK: Okay, okay, they were a fine team. I'll accept that. Did you have a favorite player?

LEWIS: This is silly.

FRANK: Favorite player!

LEWIS: Bradshaw.

(FRANK makes a buzzer sound.)

FRANK: Wrong answer!

LEWIS: What's wrong with—?

FRANK: There is no way you're going to come in here and tell me that the man you idolized was Terry fucking Bradshaw.

LEWIS: That's what I'm telling you.

FRANK: No fucking way.

LEWIS: Why is that so strange?

FRANK: What were you doing idolizing a white boy?

LEWIS: Race had nothing to do with it.

FRANK: Race has everything to do with it.

LEWIS: Not to me.

FRANK: You expect me to believe that?

LEWIS: Believe what you want.

FRANK: See, I'd feel you if you'd said Mean Joe Greene or Franco Harris. But Terry Fucking Bradshaw? Get the fuck out of here.

LEWIS: Why is that so hard to—?

FRANK: I mean, not only was he a cracker, but he tried too fucking hard.

LEWIS: What?

FRANK: He tried too hard to be liked.

LEWIS: You think so.

FRANK: Shit, yeah! I played against the motherfucker—always out there signing autographs, waving to the fans, grinnin' that dumb-ass Louisiana grin. Not me. Game day came: I had focus. I didn't have no time for sideline theatrics. You've got to keep your eyes open out there, or you'll get wrecked. Shit, you'll get wrecked anyway—one way or another.

LEWIS: Sometimes you're the bug; sometimes you're the windshield.

FRANK: I was never the bug.

LEWIS: No, but it's the law of the jungle out there, isn't it?

FRANK: Eat or be eaten, that's right! And on the football field, you got a license to kill. Who needs knives and pistols anymore? I say ban them all; give everybody a helmet and a pair of cleats. But see, the rules have all changed. It's not like it was. The game's been tainted by all these watered-down rules. I mean, no roughing the passer...? Don't hit the receiver while he's in mid-air...? What's that all about?

LEWIS: If those rules had been in place when you injured Lyle Turner—

FRANK: Then we wouldn't be having this conversation. See, what you're talking about is the line.

LEWIS: What line?

FRANK: Between taking a man down and putting him down—permanently. Tell me where it is and then we can talk. From a young age they train you do something and then suddenly it's out of bounds. All I know how to do is play—to grab, to tackle, to smash, to stomp. I can't tell you about the physics of the thing—you know, bodies in motion, rates of acceleration, mass over whatever the fuck they use to calculate impact. The thing is, once you cross that invisible line between being hurt and being injured—the one nobody can seem to locate—they say, "Oh, you went too far. You're a bad man. You have to be punished." But what I want to know is, where is that line exactly?

LEWIS: I don't know.

FRANK: Nobody does. But that's what the game is: kill the man with the ball. Take that away and football goes away.

LEWIS: The game will never go away—too much money in it.

FRANK: See, that's something you know about. Anyway, what difference does it make? The owners and fans are all a bunch of hypocrites: "Don't let him catch that pass. Draw blood," they say, "hurt the man." Hell, they were cheering me right after I hit Lyle Turner. I did what they expected me to do, what they wanted me to do, what they paid me to do.

LEWIS: You did your job.

FRANK: I did my job.

(LEWIS turns on his phone recorder again.)

LEWIS: Do you plan on apologizing?

FRANK: What?

LEWIS: You know. To Lyle Turner on Super Bowl Sunday?

FRANK: Why the hell should I?

LEWIS: Because there are some who'd say you owe him an apology—an explanation, at least. There is an injured man to whom you have never made amends.

FRANK: Is that what you want?

LEWIS: This isn't about what I want—

FRANK: It sure would make good TV, wouldn't it? But real life doesn't always work out like that. Look, I don't know what you think you're going to get on Super Bowl Sunday, but it might not be what you imagine—

LEWIS: We're paying you $100,000.

FRANK: You're going to pay me 250, and here's how it's going to go: I show up; Lyle shows up. I shake the man's hand and wish him well. You motherfuckers take a few pictures and plaster them on every website you can. You get big ratings, which translate into millions of dollars. Everybody's happy.

LEWIS: That's not good enough.

FRANK: Says who?

LEWIS: I told you that this interview is on our terms, not yours.

(LEWIS holds up the contract.)

FRANK: Just like that you want me to sign my life away.

LEWIS: We're not exacting a pound of flesh, Mr. Baker.

FRANK: You can't just spring this shit on me.

LEWIS: I represent the only network that gives a flying fuck about any of this. Most fans today don't know who the hell you are. You're a dinosaur. Sure, you still make the papers from time to time. But these days, all they write about are your financial problems. Now, I want to make this work, but a handshake won't cut it. This contract provides us the insurance we require— that you will be completely forthright about the incident that injured Mr. Turner. If you can't give me this, the network has nothing to gain by interviewing the two of you.

FRANK: You're getting one of the biggest sports stories of all time.

LEWIS: With a participant who refuses to talk about it. This is about viewership, exposure. And in the end, I'm all that stands between millions of people seeing you, and nothing.

FRANK: That's fucking blackmail.

LEWIS: No, it's a business arrangement.

FRANK: I want to talk to somebody else.

LEWIS: What?

FRANK: I'm going over your head.

LEWIS: I don't think so.

FRANK: Sure, I got plenty of friends at CBS. Who's your boss?

LEWIS: My boss—

FRANK: What's your boss's name? I want to speak to him.

LEWIS: My boss is a—it's a "she," okay? She's a female.

FRANK: Give me *her* fucking name!

LEWIS: I'm not giving you her—

FRANK: I'll find it myself then.

LEWIS: How?

FRANK: I know people.

LEWIS: Why can't you just admit you're scared?

FRANK: What?

LEWIS: This whole TV interview idea is scaring the shit out of you.

FRANK: Are you kidding me?

LEWIS: You can admit that, can't you? You have cold feet.

FRANK: I've never had cold feet in my life.

LEWIS: Except when it comes to Lyle Turner.

FRANK: Did you read about it—about what happened that day?

LEWIS: I know what happened.

FRANK: I'm asking did you read about it—the reports?

LEWIS: I didn't have to read about it.

FRANK: I thought you did your research.

LEWIS: I do my research—

FRANK: You need some context.

LEWIS: I know the context—

FRANK: Bullshit!

LEWIS: I saw it.

FRANK: Watching a game on television isn't the same as—!

LEWIS: I didn't see it on TV—

FRANK: Then you don't know nothin'!

LEWIS: I was there!

FRANK: What?

LEWIS: I mean I…it felt like I was—

FRANK: Hold on!

LEWIS: Get your hands off me!

FRANK: I want to know what you meant when you said you were there.

LEWIS: I misspoke.

FRANK: No, you didn't. Who the fuck are you?

LEWIS: My name is Lewis Turner. Lyle Turner is my father.

FRANK: Your father. Why didn't you say something?

LEWIS: I thought I could draw a clear line.

FRANK: The lines are never clear, I told you that. You might think they are, but…

LEWIS: This is different.

FRANK: Yeah, this is different. How old were you—you know, when it went down?

LEWIS: What difference does it make—?

FRANK: Answer the question.

LEWIS: I was ten.

FRANK: What did you see?

LEWIS: I saw him lying there, like, like he'd been euthanized. And there you were, towering above him like a wild ape, looking down at him to see what you'd done. From the sideline, I couldn't really see your expression; all I could see were the whites of your eyes inside the helmet...After that it was just chaos on the sideline, and somebody—one of the players—had the presence of mind to block my view of the field. Then my mother arrived and she, she took me away...

FRANK: That's some hard shit there.

LEWIS: It is what it is. Funny, but that's the first time I've ever told anybody that, and you're the last person in the world I thought I'd be telling it to.

FRANK: You hate my guts, don't you?

LEWIS: I don't want to get into this.

FRANK: We're in it, boy.

LEWIS: Don't call me that.

FRANK: I didn't mean anything—

LEWIS: Sure you did, Frank. That's what you do. You keep people in check. That's what you did on the field; that's what you're trying to do now.

FRANK: All I'm asking is whether you hate me. Not the kid that saw his daddy being carted off on a stretcher, but the man who's had twenty years to think about it.

LEWIS: What I think of you, Mr. Baker, has no bearing on our meeting today. I'm here representing CBS; that is all.

FRANK: Yeah, and that's a clear conflict of interest.

LEWIS: I won't let personal matters interfere with our business arrangement.

FRANK: We have no arrangement. There will be no arrangement.

LEWIS: This can still work.

FRANK: But how do I know whether you can perform a business transaction like this honestly and fairly.

LEWIS: You'll have to take me at my word.

FRANK: Not good enough.

LEWIS: It'll have to be. I'm a professional. I am able to leave out any personal bias—

FRANK: You expect me to believe that—

LEWIS: Whether you do or whether you don't—

FRANK: Uh huh, uh huh—

LEWIS: Certainly, when you were a player there were moments when you had personal... feelings about someone.

FRANK: Not the same thing: You run the football and break through to the secondary, I make you pay; you go over the middle and I'm nearby, I make you pay. But I harbor no ill will before or after that whistle blows.

LEWIS: That's a lie.

FRANK: Is it? See, you may think you know football, but you don't truly understand the game. Hell yes, I'm charged up—I'm excited. Maybe I even get off on it a little, like you said. But I never, ever made it personal. That takes a special discipline—one that as a son you cannot have!

LEWIS: You got anything harder to drink...?

FRANK: What'd you have in mind?

LEWIS: Vodka.

FRANK: We can do that. Help yourself.

(LEWIS gets up, pours the drink, and drinks it.)

LEWIS: What about you? Oh right, you're not a drinker.

FRANK: Pour me a double-rum.

LEWIS: You're serious.

FRANK: Do I look like I'm joking? I want a fucking drink, Lewis.

(LEWIS hands a drink to FRANK, who raises his glass.)

LEWIS: To new beginnings!

FRANK: New beginnings.

LEWIS: Wait a minute. Aren't all beginnings new?

FRANK: Probably—that's what makes them beginnings, isn't it?

LEWIS: To beginnings, then!

(They clink and drink.)

LEWIS: How's it taste?

FRANK: Like an old suit, you know, that still fits— familiar, comfortable. How does yours taste?

LEWIS: Like the one I had ten minutes before I got here.

FRANK: You like your drink.

LEWIS: I drink when I'm nervous.

FRANK: You nervous?

LEWIS: Lot of buildup.

FRANK: Butterflies before the big game.

LEWIS: Something like that. You have a reputation.

FRANK: I'm just a man, same as you, same as your father.

LEWIS: Still, you'll agree that you cultivated an image of yourself as more monster than man.

FRANK: I never looked at it like that.

LEWIS: That's how it often came off.

FRANK: You can see that I'm no monster, Lewis.

LEWIS: Players feared you.

FRANK: What you call fear I call respect.

LEWIS: They didn't call you "Assassin" because they respected you.

FRANK: Nobody ever called me Assassin, [period].

LEWIS: At least not until your book came out in the early '80s.

FRANK: That's right.

LEWIS: The publisher made the name up to sell books, but it stuck.

FRANK: You know your shit.

LEWIS: It's what I do.

(LEWIS holds up a liquor bottle; FRANK nods his assent. LEWIS tosses the bottle to FRANK, who catches it.)

FRANK: Two won't kill me.

LEWIS: That's too bad.

FRANK: Listen to me: Mistakes have been made in the past. Things that—you know—things that could've been said—

LEWIS: You're talking to the wrong man—

FRANK: You're the right man.

LEWIS: I don't think so.

FRANK: Listen: the son does not have to inherit the burdens of his father.

LEWIS: It's the sins of his father…

FRANK: Whatever you want to call them.

LEWIS: That's what they're called.

FRANK: I say the best medicine is to take a couple of deep breaths, get our heads straight, and watch the game—

LEWIS: The game's over. Look at the score.

FRANK: It's not over! Didn't you see that pass? The Ravens are moving, but damn, Patriots can't let a guy get away with that.

LEWIS: Sometimes there's nothing you can do.

FRANK: There's always something the defender can do. See, it's all in the eyes when you're a safety.

LEWIS: What are you talking about?

FRANK: What?

LEWIS: What are you talking about—the eyes?

FRANK: I'm talking about playing the game the way it should be played. See, the rookie mistake is taking your eyes off.

LEWIS: Off the—what—off the ball...?

FRANK: Off *his* eyes.

LEWIS: Whose?

FRANK: The receiver, the wide out, the skinny son of a bitch trying to burn your ass and score a touchdown!

LEWIS: I don't get it.

FRANK: That's why nobody drafted you. Now, pretend there's a receiver. Imagine he's going out for the ball. It's a long bomb, a perfect spiral, and you see it there, floating toward you. You're watching the ball come toward you, I'm facing you—we're running at full speed, mind you—and you know where I'm looking?

LEWIS: At the quarterback?

FRANK: No, nigga, I'm looking in your eyes. Because if I turn toward the ball and away from you, you know where you'll be...?

LEWIS: The end zone?

FRANK: That's right, baby, and that's not where I want you! I'm looking in your eyes because they tell me where the ball is. And when it's nearly on you, your pupils are gonna get wide, like you've just seen a ghost—or better yet, like Halle Berry just dropped her bath towel; she's standing there dripping wet, and she wants to ride your dick. You got me?

LEWIS: I got you.

FRANK: It's in the eyes, Lewis. Your eyes don't lie.

LEWIS: Neither do yours.

(FRANK turns away.)

FRANK: We're not talking about me.

LEWIS: Sure, we are, Frank. This is all about you—the TV appearance, the money, the reconciliation.

FRANK: You got it all wrong.

LEWIS: Do I?

FRANK: This isn't about me; it's about us. I want what you want.

LEWIS: And what do I want, Frank?

FRANK: You want me to sign your little contract.

LEWIS: Yes, but I also want to know how you hit a man.

FRANK: You what?

LEWIS: I want to know how you hit a man. You knew how to put guys on the carpet—lay them out so they couldn't get up. That's what I want to know.

FRANK: What are you talking about?

LEWIS: I need to know how you hit a man.

FRANK: I can't show you that.

LEWIS: What, you forgot…?

FRANK: Forgot? No, I didn't forget. That shit's in me, boy.

LEWIS: So, what's the problem?

FRANK: You're kidding me, right?

LEWIS: I'm not.

FRANK: What makes you think I'd reveal something like that to someone like you?

LEWIS: Someone like me...?

FRANK: I mean, you might have the brains to make it through Howard, but you just don't have the, the wherewithal, the, the imagination to take this kind of shit in. Even if I did think you could handle it, this is my genie in the bottle, baby—my secret formula, my special sauce. It's Top Secret. If I wrote it down, they'd have to redact this shit. Anyway, what good's it going to do you? You don't play; you hardly watch.

LEWIS: Do you blame me?

FRANK: I don't blame you—

LEWIS: Then show me. You owe me this. For all those games I didn't get to see him play; for all the touchdowns I didn't see him make; for all the championships...like the one on TV tonight. You owe me, Frank. Now, I want to know how to hit a man, and you're going to show me.

FRANK: You've got some balls, I'll give you that. So, you really want to know the secret of how I hit a man?

LEWIS: I do.

FRANK: And you really think you can handle what I have to put down?

LEWIS: I know I can.

FRANK: Well then, Lewis Turner, today is your lucky day. See, I played professional football in the NFL for twelve seasons, but what you may not know about me is that I am really a teacher, a healer, a uniter. You ready for this? The secret is…Well, the secret is there is no secret. Hitting a man is the easy part. They don't draft you because they think you're smart; they draft your ass because you're dumb enough to put your head down and lunge your entire body at a total stranger—hit a man, knock him out, put him down like a lame fucking horse. You got this string bean wideout coming across the middle all exposed and open. All you have to do is stand there and wait—bake a cake or something, set the timer. But once it comes high noon and that long-legged cocksucker comes into your kitchen, Bam! Lights out! But that's at the end. It all starts with the snap. You know what a snap is, right?

LEWIS: Don't insult me.

FRANK: Alright then, the play is about to start, Hallelujah! Come on.

LEWIS: Come on what?

(FRANK swigs his drink.)

FRANK: Line up, line up. Maybe you never played, but you know what it looks like. You want some answers; I'm going to give them to you. Move that chair. Take off your jacket.

(LEWIS moves the arm chair out of the way. FRANK rolls up his sleeves.)

FRANK: Now line up.

LEWIS: Where?

FRANK: Right here, right here, this is the line—across here. This is the line.

(He draws an invisible line with his finger to show LEWIS where to stand. LEWIS stands in front of FRANK in a loose receiver stance, waiting for the snap.)

LEWIS: Like this?

FRANK: Hell, yes! Now, here we go. First one to cry is a sissy. We'll do it in slow motion. You ready?

LEWIS: Ready.

FRANK: Blue 82…Blue 82…set, hut-hut!

(LEWIS doesn't move.)

FRANK: Move, son! You're going out for the ball.

LEWIS: But you didn't say "hike."

FRANK: I did the hike right there!

LEWIS: But you didn't say "hike."

FRANK: You sure you went to Howard?

LEWIS: What?

FRANK: Never mind. Keep going.

LEWIS: Blue 80… Blue 80… set, hike!

(LEWIS slowly walks forward.)

FRANK: These days I can only play with you for the first
    five yards. After that it's hands off. But when I started,
    all bets were off. I ride your ass, tangle you up. Little
    slaps—short and sweet like—get the receiver all nerv-
    ous, off his game, so even if the ball does get thrown
    his way he's already off balance, out of tune. You
    okay?

LEWIS: I'm okay.

FRANK: It's alright if you got the jitters a little, 'cause you're playing with *The Man* now. You're playing with the Assassin. Now, keep going.

(LEWIS walks.)

FRANK: So, you know, I'm waiting for you, right? Lurking in the woods like a fucking tiger, waiting for just the right moment to pounce.

LEWIS: And that moment is…

FRANK: The ball.

LEWIS: Right, the ball.

FRANK: I'm waiting for the ball to be thrown and when it comes—Smash! Pow! Lights out! I liked to give it right up here.

(FRANK slowly moves his forearm up into the chin and throat area of LEWIS.)

FRANK: See, right here.

LEWIS: Uh huh.

FRANK: Good. You with me?

LEWIS: I'm…I'm with you…

FRANK: Keep going. Now, look for the ball.

(LEWIS looks for the ball.)

FRANK: QB's pumping, he's throwing; here it comes!

LEWIS: I got it; I got it!

(LEWIS, into it now, looks for ball; FRANK lowers his shoulder and drives LEWIS into the wall, hard. LEWIS screams in surprise and pain. After hitting the wall, he sinks to the floor and moans.)

FRANK: How'd you like that, motherfucker?!

LEWIS: What the fuck are you doing…?!

FRANK: I'm playing, man.

LEWIS: You're out of your fucking mind!

FRANK: You alright.

LEWIS: Shit!

FRANK: Let's do it again. Come on.

LEWIS: Go to hell!

FRANK: I didn't hit you that hard.

LEWIS: Yes, you did!

FRANK: I hardly touched you.

LEWIS: You drunk, fucking asshole!

FRANK: Hey, watch your mouth, boy.

LEWIS: This isn't the NFL.

FRANK: You can say that again.

LEWIS: Jesus!

FRANK: You wanted me to show you; I showed you. Hey, when you talk to your pop you can share war stories now, right?

LEWIS: You sick fuck!

(FRANK, riled, aggressively moves toward LEWIS. The room phone rings. FRANK stops, moves back to phone, and picks it up.)

FRANK *(Into phone)*: Hello? Oh, yeah, we're fine. I fell, that's all. Everything's okay now. Yeah, we'll keep it down.

(FRANK hangs up.)

FRANK: Nothing broken, come on.

LEWIS: How do you know?

FRANK: I know what broken bones sound like. Can you move your arm?

LEWIS: I don't know!

FRANK: I'll get you some ice.

LEWIS: Forget it.

FRANK: Let me help you.

LEWIS: You're 20 years too late.

FRANK: Is that a fact?

LEWIS: Yeah. The fact is it was a dirty hit. The fact is you were a dirty player. And then you weren't even man enough to see him.

FRANK: I did see him!

LEWIS: Where—at the hospital?

FRANK: I didn't see him at the hospital. I tried, but your family wouldn't let me in.

LEWIS: Then when?

FRANK: It was years later.

LEWIS: When?

FRANK: Years later… I was down in Springfield visiting some family. You know what it's like: first two days is all hugs and high fives, but by the third day you just want to get the fuck out of the house. I needed to take a drive. So, I rented a car and got myself lost on purpose, figured I'd find a spot to have a sandwich or something. I bought an Al Green cassette in the local drug store, and, well, that shit's so good I just kept on driving. I always hated Chicago in the winter, man. The breeze—that hawk—that comes off the lake will cut your ass down, but summer's good driving weather almost anywhere you go. And by the time *Love and Happiness* came on I was driving through the South Side. I parked the car and walked the neighborhood; I knew the address: Maple Street—easy to remember because it made me think of syrup, and I got a sweet tooth. The number stuck in my head too. It was the year they held the first Super Bowl.

LEWIS: 1967…

FRANK: 1967 Maple Street. Once I found it I just stared at that house. It looked like all the others on the block—ordinary, a little worse for wear. Suddenly, I heard something—a tapping sound. I ignored it; it wasn't for me. But it kept going, this rapping. It would stop for maybe five seconds and then start up again. The house had this enclosed porch, and it took me a minute to see it, but I saw this fist banging on the window. My first instinct was to get the fuck out of there—get in the car and drive back to Springfield. But what was I supposed to do? I was here. I climbed the steps and stood in front of the door. The banging got faster and louder so I...I...put my hand on the door. It was open. Lyle was just sitting there on the porch in his wheelchair. He invited me in. I tried not to look at him too much—didn't want to make him self-conscious. It's hard to look at another man when he's...I know I wouldn't like it. Nobody wants to be pitied. I asked him how he was feeling, and he said, "Doing fine. Take each day as it comes, brother." So, I just pulled up a chair and sat next to him looking out the porch window onto Maple Street—cars coming and going, somebody out walking a dog—watching the world go by. I kind of lost track of time. A car pulled up in front of the house. It was this beat up green station wagon—old-fashioned like, wood paneling on the side.

LEWIS *(Overlapping with FRANK):* Wood paneling on the side.

FRANK: Your mother took some groceries out of the back, and then came up the steps. I felt my stomach drop. I turned to Lyle; we looked at each other for a minute. I wanted to say something important, something lasting, but all I could think to say was, "Take care of yourself, Lyle." Then I was out the back door before your mother reached the porch. But as soon as I hit the sidewalk again he banged on the window one more time—just once—this short kind of sound: "Bang!" It was probably his way of saying goodbye, but on the drive back I kept reading more into, you know? Maybe he was trying to tell me something more. Like, I don't know, Godspeed, or—

LEWIS: Or fuck you.

FRANK: Hey, I showed up! I showed up. In those days, I hardly even showed up for my own family—my wife used to call me the invisible man I'd be gone so much.

LEWIS: How is Evelyn these days, and the girls? Oh, that's right, things didn't work out. Still, thirty-three years is a pretty good run.

FRANK: That's none of your business. The bottom line is I showed up for your pop. That's what people that play the game do for one another. You wouldn't understand. Now, what are we going to do about this thing, Lewis?

LEWIS: What thing?

FRANK: The thing we're here to do—the big reunion, the big mea culpa.

LEWIS: That depends on you.

FRANK: What are you talking about, boy?

LEWIS: Don't call me "boy." Now, as I told you, I can make this happen. I can give you Super Bowl Sunday.

FRANK: Then give it to me.

LEWIS: Not until I can guarantee that you're willing to offer something substantial.

(LEWIS rotates his arm, still in pain.)

FRANK: What's wrong with your arm?

LEWIS: You drove me into a wall.

FRANK: Oh, we was just playing.

LEWIS: Is that what you call it?

FRANK: That's what it was.

LEWIS: And first one to cry is a sissy, right? I'm not going to tell anybody at CBS about this, if that's what you're worried about.

FRANK: 'Cause why?

LEWIS: Because despite what you think, I'm a man, Frank.

FRANK: I never said you weren't a man.

LEWIS: I think you did.

FRANK: You're making shit up.

LEWIS: Sign the fucking contract.

(FRANK picks up the contract; LEWIS holds up a pen.)

FRANK: Lyle has to sign this, too, right?

LEWIS: He will.

FRANK: And he'll be in an ocean of legal shit if he doesn't get his ass to Miami in two weeks, right?

LEWIS: Take the pen.

FRANK: Let me read it first.

LEWIS: I thought you didn't read contracts.

FRANK: I'm making an exception. You got some dudes in the NFL who don't read their contracts, and they get their asses burned—end up eating out of tin cans and sleeping in bus terminals. Not me, man; I read my contracts.

LEWIS: It's not really necessary.

FRANK: Shut the fuck up. *(He reads.)* What's this?

(He points to a stipulation in the contract.)

LEWIS: It's what you're agreeing to.

FRANK: Which is what exactly?

LEWIS: In your new book—

FRANK: New book? What are you talking about? That's not published yet. How'd you get a copy of that?

LEWIS: You emailed it to me, remember?

FRANK: Oh, yeah…

LEWIS: You don't even mention him. In almost 240 pages, there's not one single shred of regret—

FRANK: I don't regret shit.

LEWIS: Mr. Turner was severely injured by what you did—

FRANK: And it's still weird to me that you call your own father "Mr. Turner." Yeah, you work for CBS and all, but that's some fucked up shit.

LEWIS: Your opinion of our relationship is none of my concern. Mr. Turner believes—

FRANK: Your father!

LEWIS: We've established that. And we were under the distinct impression that this meeting on national television was, like you said, meant to be a mea culpa—a selfless act of contrition for an act of brutal violence.

FRANK: That's between me and him if—and only if—he gets his ass to that TV show.

LEWIS: But you plan to profit from it.

FRANK: What difference does that make?

LEWIS: How can he trust that you're being honest, that you're doing this because you feel true remorse, if you're getting paid?

FRANK: He's getting paid for the interview too.

LEWIS: That's not what I mean. The CBS exposure will likely land you a book contract; people will buy your book; and you will receive royalties. That's payment. Now, we'll let you publish your book, but it must be revised to contain an apology.

FRANK: Oh, you'll let me, huh?

LEWIS: That's right.

FRANK: The man can't do this to me.

LEWIS: No one has done anything to you.

FRANK: There's no reason we both can't get what we want. So, they announce I wrote a book—so what? All I'm asking is that—

LEWIS: You're in no position to ask for anything.

FRANK: Like hell I'm not! I've been prisoner to this son of a bitch for 20 fucking years. I have the right to get what I want out of this too.

LEWIS: That's not how we see it.

FRANK: That's how I see it. This is about me, now. Me! I should be in the Goddamn Hall of Fame! You know it's true. But anything you ever hear about me always comes back to what happened—nothing about my number of tackles or interceptions or years as an All-Pro—always about how I crippled a man.

LEWIS: Well, didn't you?

FRANK: But Super Bowl Sunday could be my chance—our chance.

LEWIS: To do what exactly? Tell me: What does my father gain by appearing with you?

FRANK: He gets paid!

LEWIS: That's not enough. If you're unwilling to guarantee a public apology in the book—on television—then—

FRANK: You're asking too much.

LEWIS: And in all these years you've given too little.

FRANK: You want more money, or something? Is that it?

LEWIS: This isn't about money—

FRANK: Everything's about money. Come on, Lewis. You want some royalties when my book hits the best-seller list, right?

LEWIS: I haven't asked for one dime—

FRANK: Not yet, but I feel it coming.

LEWIS: All I want is for you to acknowledge your part—

FRANK: You're just a greedy little fucker like all the rest.

LEWIS: You don't know me.

FRANK: And I don't want to know you. I just want a fair hearing.

LEWIS: You don't deserve one.

FRANK: What gives you the right to judge me?

LEWIS: He's dying!

FRANK: What do you want me to do about it?

LEWIS: I want you to give a shit, Frank. Don't you get it? Bradshaw was nothing compared to you. You had the tight mustache, the badass 'fro, and you didn't take shit from anybody. Hell no, man, you doled it out like poison candy. And those uniforms: The silver and black, the pirate logo on the helmet. What little kid doesn't want to be a pirate, right? My father brought home Patriot merchandise all the time, but I didn't want it. Finally, he gave in and for my birthday he bought me your jersey with the number 32 and B-A-K -E-R spelled out between the back shoulders. I wore it for three weeks straight; I slept in the Goddamn thing. They couldn't get it off me. Two months later I was wearing it on the sidelines of a preseason game between the New England Patriots and the Oakland Raiders. It was only an exhibition game—it was meaningless—but it was the only game I cared about. You know why? Because I knew you would be there. My father told me he didn't know you very well, but he said he'd try to introduce the two of us when it was over. He never got the chance.

FRANK: Jesus…

LEWIS: I was wearing the jersey in the ambulance on the way to the hospital. Nobody paid any attention; I forgot I was wearing it until my mother took me home that night. We got in the front door and suddenly she was just standing there, looking at me. "Take that off," she said. I didn't know what she meant. She slapped me across the face. "Take it off, I said!" I took it off, and then it was gone. I wanted to hate you, but I couldn't. So, I hated myself. Jesus, I'd been raised to love the game for what it was: the bigger the plays, the harder the hitting—the better. See, football gave my father a life—opportunities beyond anything he'd ever dreamed of. And then…

FRANK: Football took it all away.

LEWIS: Just like that.

FRANK: Just like that. It could've happened to anybody.

LEWIS: It happened to me. He could die any day. And when he does, you know what the newspapers are going to say? They're going to say that you never lifted a finger to help him, never even acknowledged...You just went on your way pretending it never happened. That will be your legacy.

FRANK: How the hell do you know what they're going to say about me?

LEWIS: Because I've already written his obituary! And I'll make damn sure that it finds its way into every newspaper in the country. That is, unless you tell me—tell him—that in the book and on Super Bowl Sunday, you'll say the words, "I'm sorry."

FRANK: Call him first.

LEWIS: What?

FRANK: Let me talk with him directly, with the man himself.

LEWIS: You'll get your chance.

FRANK: I mean right now.

LEWIS: I don't think that's such a good idea.

FRANK: Why not? I'm doing you a solid, and now you're supposed to return the favor. It's called good manners. Call him and tell him that despite all the bullshit the two of you put me through tonight I'm willing to make this peace offering by signing your little—

LEWIS: I'll tell him later.

FRANK: Tell him now.

LEWIS: It's not necessary.

FRANK: Yeah, it is.

LEWIS: Why?

FRANK: 'Cause you're a sneaky fuck, and I don't trust you. Make the call, Lewis.

(LEWIS, injured arm still tender, reaches for the cell phone in his jacket pocket. He dials.)

FRANK: Talk to him, man to man, father to son.

LEWIS *(Into phone)*: Hi, it's Lewis. Can you put my dad on the phone? Hi, pop, how are you feeling? It's, it's, I don't know, 8:30…I'll be home soon…Yeah, he's, he's right here…I did. I explained everything to him in detail and, well, at first, he was a little reluctant—

FRANK: That's an understatement.

LEWIS *(Into phone)*: But yes, he's agreed to abide by our terms—

FRANK: I'm going to sign it, brother!

LEWIS *(To FRANK)*: Can you let me handle this, please?

FRANK: Sure, yeah.

LEWIS *(Into phone)*: He seems very serious. He really does—

(FRANK grabs the phone from LEWIS' hand.)

LEWIS: Hey!

FRANK *(Into phone)*: I mean it, Lyle—

LEWIS *(To FRANK)*: Give it to me—

FRANK *(Into phone)*: I really do—

LEWIS *(To FRANK)*: He won't talk to you—

FRANK *(Into phone)*: What do you say—?

LEWIS *(To FRANK)*: Give it to me—!

FRANK *(Into phone)*: Lyle—!

LEWIS *(To FRANK)*: He won't talk to you—

FRANK *(Into phone)*: Lyle—?

LEWIS *(To FRANK)*: I'm telling you—

FRANK *(Into phone)*: Are you there—?

LEWIS *(To FRANK)*: Give it—!

FRANK: What the fuck is going on, Lewis?

LEWIS: He, he must have hung up…

FRANK: He didn't hang up; he wasn't there.

LEWIS: I was just talking to him.

FRANK: I don't think you were.

LEWIS: Of course I was.

FRANK: Don't lie to me, motherfucker! Don't lie to me! Does he even know you're here? Does he know anything about this?

LEWIS: Yes.

FRANK: You're a lying piece of shit. What else are you, Lewis?

LEWIS: I don't know what you mean—

FRANK: Do you really work for CBS, or what?

LEWIS: No.

FRANK: What about the contract?

LEWIS: I got it online.

(Enraged, FRANK swings his cane, knocking objects off coffee table. He seethes and tries to compose himself.)

FRANK: You just wanted to meet the man that crippled your daddy. Is that it? Well, you can say one thing for yourself, Lewis Turner: tonight, you finally faced the beast.

LEWIS: When are you going to face it, Frank?

FRANK: What do you want me to say? Do I wish things had been different? What do you think? Do I wish your daddy could still walk? I do. But I won't apologize for the way I played. See, if I do that, well… Let's just say we all live with a lot of shit inside us, but it's a choice you make. And when death is staring you in the face, you can either cling to it, or move away. I chose to move away a long time ago.

LEWIS: But I couldn't move away. I had to be there. I had to be a son. I've been following your career and life for years—the statistics, the championships, the retirement, the foreclosures, bankruptcy: your slow decline from legend to has-been.

FRANK: Don't call me a has-been—!

LEWIS: That's what you are, Frank.

FRANK: I ought to break your fucking neck!

LEWIS: Three weeks ago, I read that you were looking to publish a new book. I knew I had to contact you—find out what was in it—but there had to be a reason. It wasn't hard: I'd offer you a Super Bowl interview, and in return you'd send me your manuscript. I read it front to back, but not one word, not one fucking word.

FRANK: You'd do the same thing in my shoes.

LEWIS: I'm not like you at all.

FRANK: Don't fool yourself. There's a little Frank Baker in everybody. It's called self-preservation.

LEWIS: It's called lying.

FRANK: You're one to fucking talk.

LEWIS: You are going to admit your part in this. Tell me now—tell me to my face—that you are responsible.

FRANK: What difference does it make?

LEWIS: It makes a difference.

FRANK: To who?

LEWIS: To me, Frank. To me.

FRANK: The hit was legal. That was a legal fucking hit—nothing wrong with that hit. Look it up. Those were the rules back then. I didn't make the rules. I did nothing wrong.

LEWIS: You destroyed his life; you destroyed my life!

FRANK: What about my life? What about my fucking life?

LEWIS: You had your life!

FRANK: You think that just because a man has use of his legs he's free? Let me tell you something, Lewis: bondage comes in a variety of forms. Your father has kept me in chains for 20 years.

LEWIS: That's bullshit!

FRANK: I can't even get a coaching job—nobody will hire me. All the shit I did—all the awards I won, all the charity work—and all anybody ever talks about is what happened to Lyle Turner.

LEWIS: What you did to Lyle Turner!

FRANK: Yeah, but see, if somebody else's father had been carried off on the gurney that day what difference would it have made to you? None. You can admit that, can't you? Nobody thinks they have to pay a price, and most of the time they don't. If things get fucked up it's always somebody else's fault. Pick a scape-goat—blame him, blame me. That's what I am: one in a long list of scapegoats for somebody else's shit. See, players get hit like that all the time, every Goddamn game, week in, week out, but they alright, they walking around. So why did *that* hit make a man a cripple? Tell me, I want to know! You think I had control over that shit? Our bodies collided, that's all. The rest wasn't up to me. Call it fate, destiny, I don't know. No, see, it wasn't me that did that to your father. It was God.

LEWIS: You believe that.

FRANK: I have to believe something. The truth is your father just didn't belong in the NFL, son. He couldn't handle it. That's why you don't hate me. Somewhere inside yourself you know it too. The truth hurts, but that's the way it is.

LEWIS: No.

FRANK: That day you got to see a real man play.

LEWIS: Don't say that.

FRANK: That day you got to see your hero put your daddy on his back like a woman. Ain't that right, boy?

(LEWIS slaps FRANK, hard, across the face.)

FRANK: It's the truth!

LEWIS: Bullshit!

(LEWIS pummels Frank. LEWIS places his elbow at FRANK's throat, much like FRANK did to LEWIS earlier.)

LEWIS: Fight back, motherfucker! Fight back!

FRANK: I can't breathe...I can't...

(LEWIS finally removes his elbow/forearm from FRANK's windpipe; FRANK collapses and gasps for air.)

LEWIS: Stand up! Stand the fuck up! What are you waiting for? Guess you just don't have it in you anymore, old man. Life is like that. One day you're able-bodied and upright; the next, you're flat on the ground, and there's a monster standing over you...

(LEWIS stands directly over FRANK.)

LEWIS: Now, I want you to beg me. Beg me!

FRANK: I ain't gonna...I ain't gonna beg...

LEWIS: He used to beg me.... "Take the pillow there. Take it, boy. Put it over my face and press down. Count to three: one-two-three." I just couldn't. He looked so fragile lying there. "Do it, Lewis. Just this once. Please, boy, please..."

FRANK: So, you thought—what—that by coming here, by negotiating some kind of reunion—some kind of apology—and bringing it to him on a silver platter—by being a good son...

LEWIS: That I could get it to stop!

FRANK: To stop...?

LEWIS: I betrayed him. And all those years I wiped his ass, brushed his teeth, got him dressed—all those years my mother struggled to feed us, keep a roof over our heads—the only thing I could think about was how things would have been different if only I hadn't been there, if only I hadn't worn your.... It sounds crazy, doesn't it?

FRANK: No.

LEWIS: And now, with the contract and the book, well, I could say, "Look, pop, look what I did. Look what I did for you, for us. I got Frank Baker to take responsibility for what happened, and to say that's he's sorry too. It can't be my fault—what happened to you, pop. It can't be my fault if...if...."

FRANK: If it's mine...

LEWIS: Yes.

(While LEWIS is turned away, FRANK picks up and signs the contract before handing it to LEWIS.)

LEWIS: I don't understand.

FRANK: Let him see it. Before it's too late…

LEWIS: There's no appearance, no TV show, no money.

FRANK: Lyle will [he'll] understand. Just do it. Please.

(LEWIS pauses, takes the signed contract, and places it in his briefcase. Voice on TV announces a Patriots win: "Ladies and gentlemen, the New England Patriots are going to the Super Bowl." LEWIS and FRANK look at the TV screen.)

FRANK: Would you look at that: Your pop's old team is going to the big game! How about one more drink?

LEWIS: I better go.

(LEWIS puts on his jacket, takes his briefcase, moves to door, and then turns back.)

LEWIS: Hey, Frank. You showed up.

FRANK: That's what men do. We show up…

(LEWIS exits; FRANK is alone. Sounds of the game return; the crowd cheers. Lights fade to black.)

END OF PLAY

Writing *Playing the Assassin* by David Robson

Playing the Assassin began with an obituary. In the summer of 2010, I came across the death notice of former NFL safety Jack Tatum. The name alone evoked my youth and early football fanaticism. As a kid, I'd been a Steelers fan and had a great fondness for my home team, the Eagles, too. Still, I knew Tatum, who'd played for the notorious Oakland Raiders, by reputation: In the 1970s, he was known as the league's hardest hitter—a steam engine of a man—and a dirty player known to take cheap shots when given the chance.

The obituary headline, though, reminded me of something else. It read, "Jack Tatum, Whose Tackle Paralyzed Player, Dies at 61." During a 1978 pre-season game, Tatum put a hit on New England Patriots wide receiver Darryl Stingley. The play looked routine, but Stingley never got up; he was permanently paralyzed from the neck down. For the next thirty years, the two men never spoke. Stingley died in 2007.The incident and its aftermath trailed Tatum like a hellhound for the rest of his life, and in death that's how his time on earth was summed up in print: as a man who had destroyed the life of someone else. That was his tragic legacy.

Some writers, when inspired, jot a few lines of verse; others create a narrative that may become a short story or novel. I have people talk to one another. I don't hear voices, mind you. I simply place people in a room together and see what happens. Thus, in the days after reading Tatum's obituary I imagined a meeting in a hotel decades after a catastrophic collision like the one between Tatum and Stingley. I changed the names and many of the details, but I wondered what might happen if a Tatum-like character tried to make one last ditch effort to reconcile with the man he injured. At the beginning I had no clue. Would the disabled man even show up? If so, what would the two say to one another? Could they ever find a way to put the past behind them? At first, it sounded like a bizarre mash-up of *Waiting for Godot* and the *Knute Rockne Story*, but on I typed.

Before I knew it, another man—able-bodied and strong—walked into my play. He was a television producer, and as he and the former NFL hitman attempted to negotiate a televised reunion, I discovered more about each of them: their strengths and weaknesses, their senses of humor, and the true reason each man had agreed to this meeting in the first place. I never set out to write a "football" play. I'm not even sure what a football play is exactly. I only knew that once the story got rolling, I had to see what happened.

Long after I'd completed the first draft of *Playing the Assassin*, a line by poet Theodore Roethke came back to me: "A man goes far to find out what he is." Life, with all its pain, joy, and in-between is a journey that, in the end, forces us to reckon with the choices we've made, our victories and our failures, our gains and our losses. Only then can we truly discover the kind of stuff we're made of. During the course of the play, my two characters, Lewis and Frank, confront each other, lie to one another, and attempt to face their demons. In doing so, they reveal their true natures and come face-to-face with who and what they are. They also hope against hope that what happens between them will change their lives, even redeem them, before it's too late.

NOTES

NOTES

www.ingramcontent.com/pod-product-compliance
Lightning Source LLC
Chambersburg PA
CBHW062009040426
42447CB00010B/1984